◁ **Bathers in the Seine,
La Grenouillère** 1869

Oil on canvas

THIS POPULAR SPOT on the
Seine was also the subject of
paintings by Monet, which is
not surprising since the two
young friends often
frequented the café-boating
place together. The broken
streaks of paint used to
describe the reflections in the
water and the loose handling
of the paint is typical of the
early Impressionist technique
which was occupying the
minds of the revolutionary
young painters. The effect is to
give the viewer an instant and
lively impression of the
location and the open air.

◁ **Riders in the Bois de Boulogne** 1873

Oil on canvas

THESE ELEGANT RIDERS belong to the period when Renoir was making a living by painting conventional, modern-life pictures for wealthy patrons, as well as doing his own experimental Impressionist work. The riders are models, playing the part of the affluent kind of people to be seen in the Bois de Boulogne. Paintings of this kind would naturally appeal to the fashionable public, the kind of people who might well have regarded Renoir's paintings of boating parties and other pursuits of ordinary people as slightly vulgar.

▷ **La Loge** 1874

Oil on canvas

THE LIFE OF FRANCE'S affluent middle classes, who had become wealthy from trade and commerce, fascinated the humbly-born Renoir. Even so, he used a Montmartre model called Nini *guele en raie* and his brother Edmond to pose for La Loge. In this artistic *tour de force* Renoir portrays a well-off woman in a box at the opera in all her finery and attended by a smart, sophisticated man-about-town. It is not difficult to imagine the kind of life this opulent couple would have led in their smart Paris flat, no doubt on one of the new tree-fringed avenues laid out by Baron Haussmann. These were the kind of people who bought Renoir's paintings and commissioned portraits from him, and he admired them as much as he depended on them for work. Despite Renoir's traditional treatment of the subject, using thin, delicate layers of colour to achieve the required effect, he exhibited *La Loge* in the first Impressionist Exhibition in 1874.

Detail

▷ **Alfred Sisley** 1874

Oil on canvas

Sisley had been a good friend of Renoir's since they met as young students at Gleyre's studio, despite their different temperaments. Sisley, though born in Paris in 1839, had English parents, and was more phlegmatic than Renoir. As his father was a well-off businessman Sisley at first did not have the financial worries of Renoir; these came later when his father died and his painting qualities were still not recognized. Though Sisley worked occasionally in England his main themes were the places where the Impressionists gathered along the Seine at Argenteuil, Bougival and Marly. Sisley died in 1899, before his work was fully recognized.

◁ **Les Grands Boulevards** 1875

Oil on canvas

THE MAKING OF the *grands boulevards* by Baron Haussmann under the orders of Napoleon III changed the face of Paris. Small medieval blocks of houses were torn down to make wide avenues criss-crossing the city, and, it was said, allowing better control of possible rioters. In fact, the *grands boulevards* became the great social centres of Paris, where the rich paraded in their horse-drawn coaches and the ordinary citizen promenaded or sat at cafés to watch the world go by. Renoir's lively picture of the boulevards preceded that of Monet, and was just one of numerous cityscapes and scenes of Parisian life Renoir painted in the 1860s and 1870s.

◁ **Roses in a
Pottery Vase** 1876

Oil on canvas

RENOIR WAS FASCINATED by
flowers, especially roses, which
in later life he grew at his
property in Cagnes so he
could paint them every day,
nourishing a passion for the
flower formed in the 1870s. In
this study of roses in a ceramic
jug Renoir was evidently
looking at the colour of the
unfolding roses as their petals
caught the light and
contrasting their soft warmth
with the cooler tones and
curves of the jug. The table on
which the vase is standing and
the background are treated in
a rather perfunctory way,
which seems to confirm that
Renoir's main interest was a
study of roses.

△ **Looking Out at the Sacré Coeur** c.1876

Oil on canvas

WHEN RENOIR and his friends were living at Batignolles he painted a series of Paris pictures. This one shows the church of Sacré Coeur on the summit of the Butte de Montmartre. At the time, this was still country outside the jurisdiction of the city, and attracted many people who wanted to avoid its laws and taxes. Today, Montmartre is totally built over but a vineyard still survives, as does an Impressionist haunt, the country inn known as Lapin à Gil – Gil's Rabbit – a reference to the inn sign painted by someone called Gil.

◁ **A Girl with a Watering-can** 1876

Oil on canvas

MADEMOISELLE LECLERE in her smart blue dress was probably the daughter of one of the rich patrons who bought Renoir's paintings. This charming portrait of her is painted with that special empathy that Renoir had with children and, quite unlike his nudes, has a very personal feeling. The child's golden hair is contrasted nicely with the green background and the blue of her dress. There is a certain stiffness about the picture which suggests the child was holding herself still with an unconscious impatience: unlike Renoir's other models, who seemed to have infinite patience, Miss Leclere would not be standing there, flowers and watering-can in hand, for very long.

▷ **Girl with a Cat** 1876

Oil on canvas

CHILDREN WITH ANIMALS featured in several of Renoir's paintings, and the theme of the girl with a cat turned up again in a painting of Julie Manet (Berthe Morisot's daughter), some ten years after this charming picture. With both paintings, Renoir took the trouble to make preliminary sketches; a sketch of this painting was put up for sale at Sotheby's in London in 1968. In the sketch, the tabby is quite a big cat; by the time the painting was finished, it had changed into a large kitten with more strongly defined tabby markings.

Detail

▷ **The Spanish Guitarist** c.1876

Oil on canvas

SPANISH MUSIC was much in fashion in Paris in the 1870s (Bizet's *Carmen* was written in 1875), with the flamenco guitar being particularly popular. Perhaps its sound had a special appeal to northern Europeans hankering after the exotic atmosphere of the southern Mediterranean. In this picture, Renoir put the sitter in what look like a matador's 'suit of lights'. He was to do the same thing some 30 years later when he painted the dealer Ambroise Vollard wearing the 'suit of lights' he had brought back after a visit to Spain.

▷ **The Moulin de la Galette** 1876

Oil on canvas

THE MOULIN DE LA GALETTE was an open-air dance-hall on the hill of Montmartre, outside the tax belt of Paris, and was a favourite meeting-place for the lower bourgeoisie of the city, who could enjoy drinking cheaply in its acacia-shaded courtyard, while meeting the opposite sex with propriety. Renoir painted the Moulin in 1876 as a *tour de force* to show off his talent to the art-loving public. Like the *Lunch of the Boating Party* a few years later, it shows his extraordinary talent for scenes composed of many people engaged in different activities. Most of the men and women in this picture were Renoir's friends and included dancers, writers and painters. Renoir painted several versions of the scene; this one is the best-known version in The Musée d'Orsay in Paris.

◁ **Moulin de la Galette
(detail)** 1876

Oil on canvas

THIS DETAIL of the Musée
d'Orsay's version of the
Moulin de la Galette in
Montmartre is interesting as a
study of how the Impressionist
technique was used by Renoir.
The brushstrokes were laid on
separately in order to give a
lively surface which emulated
light reflected off an object
and colours were used pure
for the best effect, instead of
mixed together as was the
custom with academic painters
whose canvases had a
fashionable brown look.
Pissarro had laid down the
basic principles for
Impressionism by
recommending that the basic
palette should be the three
primary colours red, yellow,
blue and the complementary
colours orange, green, violet,
the effect of which was created
by placing brushstrokes of the
primary colours side by side
and allowing their mixture to
take place in the viewer's eye.

◁ **Portrait of Victor Chocquet** 1876

Oil on canvas

VICTOR CHOCQUET was a customs official and art-lover who championed the Impressionist painters at a time when they had little public support. He met Renoir at the unsuccessful Hôtel Drouot exhibition in 1876 and first commissioned him to paint a portrait of his wife. This portrait of Chocquet was painted a year later. Renoir enjoyed the company of other men and sometimes complained of being bored at home with too much female company. In this portrait there is an evident rapport between artist and sitter whom Renoir shows as a sensitive, intellectual, good-humoured man.

◁ **Madame Charpentier and her Children** 1878

Oil on canvas

WITH THIS PAINTING, Renoir achieved what he had set his heart on: acceptance by the Salon. The painting was a big success at the 1879 Salon and brought him the patronage of wealthy people and the financial security needed to carry on with his experimental Impressionism. M. Georges Charpentier was a publisher and he and his wife had a notable *salon* of intellectuals. Renoir visited them in their seaside home at Pourville, near Dieppe, where he painted by the sea and met Paul Berard, an embassy secretary who also commissioned work from him.

Detail

▷ **La Place Pigalle** c.1880

Oil on canvas

AT VARIOUS TIMES in his life Renoir took a leaf out of his painter friends' notebooks; with Monet he painted a scene at La Grenouillère on the Seine, and after visiting Cézanne at Aix he painted Mont Sainte-Victoire. Here, he seems to be doing a Degas street scene: the people hurrying in and out of the picture give it the snapshot quality of a Degas composition, though one glance at the face of the girl in the foreground is enough to tell you that it is by Renoir. The scene is in the Place Pigalle in Montmartre, a quarter of Paris which was a great centre of entertainment, even in Renoir's day.

◁ **Girl Wearing a Straw Hat**

Oil on canvas

THE CHARMING YOUNG LADIES wearing attractive hats who featured in so many of Renoir's paintings seem to be permanently suspended in a world of innocence and insouciance, a world where peace and happiness reigned and daily life was full of jolly events. To many of his contemporaries, Renoir was an 'escapist' painter, looking at the pleasant side of life rather than investigating its seedier or more intellectually demanding aspects.

Not for Renoir the tired dancing girls and prostitutes who were the subject of so many of Toulouse-Lautrec's paintings, or the intellectual wrestling with form and content which marked so much of Cézanne's work.

Detail

▷ **Railway Bridge at Chatou** 1891

Oil on canvas

RENOIR DID NOT PAINT many landscapes; but this is a charming exception with the railway bridge hiding behind the flowering chestnut trees and a figure, perhaps the artist himself, standing in the gap in the fence with the river beyond. It was painted at Chatou, one of several places on the Seine out of Paris – Bougival and Asnières were others – which were to become famous as a result of the Impressionists work there.

◁ **The Luncheon of the Boating Party** 1881

Oil on canvas

RENOIR'S FRIENDS admired this lively painting of a boating party in which some of them appear: the lady with the dog, for instance, is Aline Charigot, later Renoir's wife. The picture was undoubtedly intended as a *tour de force,* and one Renoir had been thinking about for some time. 'I have been itching to do it for a long time,' he wrote to Paul Berard. 'I am not getting any younger and I did not want to delay this little feast.' In fact, Renoir was nearly 40 and his best painting years were to come. But on the threshold of middle age he was beginning to feel intimations of mortality – or, at least, a need for a change of direction.

◁ **Young Girl in a Straw Hat**

Oil on canvas

HATS AND ABUNDANT HAIR often appear in Renoir's paintings, framing or half-hiding the face and giving an air of mystery to what might otherwise be rather ordinary features. In some cases, Renoir is clearly interested in the model, especially if they are his family or friends; in others, as with his nudes, the model is simply an object that starts a train of thought about the painting. The model was also essential, Renoir said, because if his ideas about the painting began to get out of hand he needed the model to bring him back to earth.

▷ Young Girl Wearing a White Hat

Oil on canvas

ANOTHER PRETTY GIRL, another pretty hat. The theme turns up again and again in Renoir's work. One of the most evocative items amongst the many relics of the artist's life in his studio at Les Collettes, his villa at Cagnes-sur-Mer, is the straw hat, its crown encircled with artificial flowers, which lies near his easel. It is as if it waits for the artist to reach out, put it on his model's head, and start another charming portrait.

◁ **Young Woman in a Fur Hat**

Oil on canvas

RENOIR ABANDONED the airs of
summer for this portrait of a
girl in a fur hat. The treatment
is simple, the absence of the
abundant hair which featured
in so many of Renoir's 'girls
with hats' pictures is also
unusual. Perhaps he was
deliberately seeking a more
severe style of drawing in line
with the classical tradition he
had come to admire so greatly.

▷ Umbrellas
(Les Parapluies) c.1886

Oil on canvas

Umbrellas was painted during
the period when Renoir was
trying to break away from his
Impressionist style and tighten
his line and structure. Visits to
Italy and to Cézanne at
L'Estaque in the south of
France had a profound effect
on him and he felt
discouraged about his previous
work. He had also decided to
work more in the studio than
outdoors because, he said,
'outdoor painting is too
complicated an affair, a kind of
painting that makes you
constantly compromise with
yourself.' *Umbrellas* is really
two paintings, for the figures
on the right are still in the
Impressionist style while the
figures on the left and the
umbrellas themselves show
Renoir's new preoccupation
with form in a Cézanne
manner. Later, Renoir
managed to fuse the two ways
of painting, creating some of
his greatest works.

▷ **Richard Wagner** 1882

Oil on canvas

IN 1881 RENOIR visited Italy,
making his first contact with
the Greek and Roman cultures
and with the work of the
Renaissance painters, which so
impressed him that he had to
re-assess the value of what he
had done so far. While in Sicily
he met the great maestro
Richard Wagner who was in
the midst of writing *Parsifal*.
The notoriously
temperamental composer
agreed to give Renoir a sitting
of 25 minutes, during which
time the painter produced this
portrait, probably the last of
the famous composer, for he
died in 1883.

▷ **Dance at Bougival** 1883

Oil on canvas

IN 1882-3 RENOIR painted three nearly life-size pictures of couples dancing. Two were the deliberately contrasted *Dance in the Country* and *Dance in the City*. The couple dancing here seem, in contrast to the other two, to be in an ambience that is neither city nor country. The pencil sketch for *Dance at Bougival* shows a much more rural pair with a girl, though wearing a long dress, less smartly turned out and the man a more clumsy and countrified character. Evidently Renoir decided to smarten them both up in the finished painting. Once again, Renoir used friends as his models. The man in all three pictures was his old friend, Paul Lhote; the girl, both here and in *Dance in the City*, was a circus acrobat called Maria Clémentine who later became famous as the artist Suzanne Valadon, mother of Maurice Utrillo.

Moulin Huet Bay, Guernsey 1883

Oil on canvas

◁ *Previous pages 44-45*

RENOIR VISITED JERSEY and Guernsey briefly in September 1883, just after the exhibition organized for him by the dealer Durand-Ruel. As he usually did when travelling, he made numerous sketches and some paintings of his surroundings, finding a certain affinity with the landscape, which resembled that of the coast of Normandy. The break in the Channel Island coincided with a hiatus in Renoir's work, about which he wrote to Durand-Ruel saying that he had reached the end of Impressionism and had come to the conclusion that he did not know how to paint or draw.

▷ Bather with Long Hair

Oil on canvas

THIS EXCEPTIONALLY fine nude shows Renoir's penchant for long hair and his artistic mastery of the nude figure. Jean Renoir once quoted his father as saying, 'It is with my brush that I make love', meaning that the act of carefully and sensitively building up the layers of paint to produce that glowing life of his nudes was an act of love for life itself. Unlike Cézanne, who explored the structure of objects, Renoir wanted to express the quality in tangible and visible things which convey a feeling of living matter. In his nudes he depicts not so much sensuality as an idealised vision of the *élan vital*.

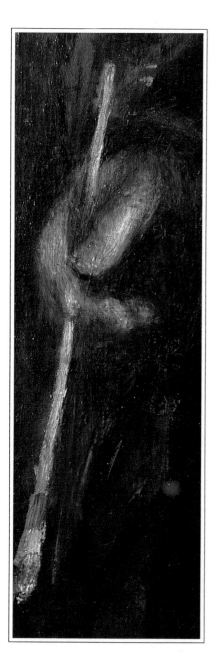

Detail

▷ **Portrait of Monet** 1875

Oil on canvas

THE PORTRAIT of Claude Monet in his midthirties was exhibited at the second Impressionist exhibition. It is not only a revealing portrait of the artist but evocative of all the young friends and companions in the new movement in painting, whose world had not yet received general acceptance by the public. Monet himself was in financial difficulties, though his letter to Manet – 'It's getting more and more difficult. Not a penny left since the day before yesterday, and no more credit at the butcher's or the baker's. You couldn't possibly send me a 20 france note by return of post. Could you?' – could have been written by several of the Impressionists of the time.

▷ **The Bathers (Les Grandes Baigneuses)** 1884-7

Oil on canvas

IT TOOK THREE YEARS of
endless sketches and
preparatory versions for
Renoir to be satisfied with this
painting, in which he was
trying to return to a more
classical line of drawing. Its
more precise, harder
modelling has been called
Renoir's *manière aigre*. The
painting was well received –
except by his friend Pissarro,
who thought that Renoir's visit
to Italy and his subsequent
attempt to change his style was
a mistake, and had led to a loss
in the colour value of the
picture. In order to tighten his
line, Renoir had studied
Ingres, and the influence of
the French classicist is visible
here.

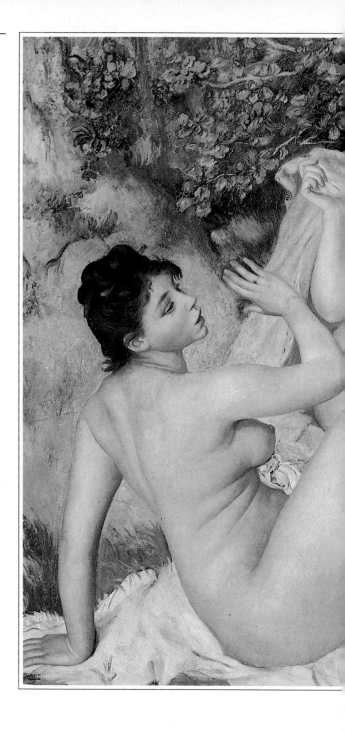

▷ **Mother and Child** 1886

Oil on canvas

THE MOTHER AND CHILD in this charming picture are Aline Renoir and Pierre. It may be coincidence but Renoir's 'Hard line' style, adopted after his visit to Italy and his discovery of such Renaissance masters as Raphael, had begun to soften at about this time. He now returned to the atmospheric style of his earlier paintings though with a more monumental form which would later become apparent in the sculpture he began doing when increasing arthritis made it difficult for him to hold a paint brush.

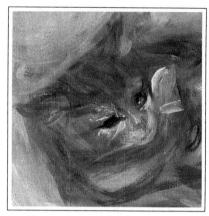

Detail

▷ **Pierre Renoir** 1890

Oil on canvas

PIERRE RENOIR was Renoir's
eldest son, born in 1885 to
Aline Charigot, Renoir's long-
time model whom he married
the year that this picture was
painted. Aline had been with
Renoir at least ten years, for
she appears in the *Luncheon of
the Boating Party* of 1880 and
had given him moral support
during his personal artistic
crisis when he had become
disillusioned with his
Impressionist style of painting
and had sought another
solution. Pierre's birth was to
inspire a delightful series of
family paintings, beginning
with one of Pierre at Aline's
breast.

▷ **Portrait of the Poet Stéphane Mallarmé**

Oil on canvas

FRENCH POETRY has always reflected philosophical ideas, particularly in the 19th century when France was in a state of political and cultural turmoil after the Napoleonic era. Mallarmé, a contemporary of Renoir, believed that poetry was the expression of the mysterious meaning of existence and gave the only form of authenticity to life on earth. In this way, he was a precursor of the existentialist idea that the only reality is the one that you are living in. Such an idea accorded well with the Impressionist aim of recording nature as actually seen. In 1891 Renoir made several engravings for the poet's book, *Pages*.

◁ **Young Girls at the Piano** c.1892

Oil on canvas

AFTER HIS MARRIAGE, Renoir seemed to discover the joys of domesticity, and from this time he would paint many paintings of his and friends' children. By 1890, Renoir had moved on from his severely linear, classical manner and had developed a technique which combined the colourfulness of Impressionism with the solidity of the old masters. In this painting of two young girls at the piano, Renoir gives a glimpse of the domestic life of his time when almost every household had a piano with brass candleholders and young sons and daughters of the bourgeoisie were encouraged to take up artistic interests such as music, singing and painting and drawing.

Gabrielle and Jean 1895

Oil on canvas

▷ *Overleaf page 58*

THE EMOTIONAL CONTENT of Renoir's domestic scenes is particularly strong in paintings of his children. This one of his second son Jean and Gabrielle gives a strong feeling of the attachment between the boy and the girl; she had joined the Renoir household at the age of 16 and had become very much one of the family as well as Renoir's favourite model.

In Renoir's close-knit family group everyone understood that painting came first in his life and there were no competing interests. Thus, all his family posed for him, though the children sometimes did so reluctantly and had to be threatened or bribed to persuade them to sit or stand still.

Girl with a fan 1880

Oil on canvas

◁ *Previous page 59*

THIS DARK-HAIRED GIRL is Alphonsine Fournaise who also posed for another Renoir portrait the year that he broke his arm and had to paint left-handed but with no ill effect on his work. The fan gives a certain Japanese flavour to the picture, an influence perhaps derived from the Japanese prints that had been much admired by other Impressionist painters, in particular van Gogh and Gauguin. The fan with its sharp diagonals and its rounded top, which echoes the shape of the girl's shoulders, makes an interesting addition to an otherwise conventional portrait pose.

▷ Young Girl Drawing

Oil on canvas

THE YOUNG GIRL in this painting, with her reddish hair and pink cheeks, bears a likeness to Renoir's youngest son, Claude. Like many painters, Renoir tended to give all his sitters a distinctive 'look'. His girls had dark hair and elongated, cat-like eyes – 'Cats are the only women who count, the most amusing to paint', Renoir once remarked to his son, Jean – and his men had romantically long hair, dark eyes and beards. Even so, his friends and family, who all sat many times for the artist, are all recognizable in their portraits.

◁ **Woman with a Rose**

Oil on canvas

THIS HEAD OF A WOMAN is in the style of the portraits of the 1870s that were making Renoir's work acceptable in the Salon and, more importantly, to the picture-buying society of Paris. Renoir's talent in producing pictures that combined academic acceptability with a new style of painting made life financially easier for him, moreso than it was for artists like Monet. It enabled him to follow his own artistic path.

△ **Women with a Rose** 1900

Oil on canvas

ROSES WERE A FAVOURITE flower for Renoir, who did fewer flower paintings than other artists of his period. The open, soft-edged petals of roses and their texture appealed to the painter, just as a woman's skin did. When combined, the two gave Renoir new inspiration and, as he told Ambroise Vollard, he found that in discovering new ways of painting the petals he also learned how to enhance his painting of the skin of his nudes.

△ **Claude Renoir Playing** 1905

Oil on canvas

CLAUDE RENOIR, known in the family as 'Coco', the third son of the painter and his wife Aline, was born in 1901 when Renoir was sixty. It was the year after Renoir's great Paris success at the Centenaire, to which he had sent 15 paintings. At last he had arrived as a painter, was accepted by the establishment and had been awarded the *Chevalier de la Légion d'Honneur.* In spite of his success, Renoir remained a simple man, attached to his family and, as he himself said, 'I feel a simple little man.' This child-like simplicity, that remained with him all his life, made his nudes so pure and his children's paintings so perceptive.

◁ **Girl Combing her Hair**

Oil on canvas

RENOIR IS BEST KNOWN for his paintings of women, often nude and usually suggesting some aspect of domestic life rather than an abstract sexuality. This young girl is performing the same sort of everyday ritual as Degas's women having baths or ironing their clothes. The Impressionists' choice of such subjects, long considered beyond the bounds of good taste in art, reflects the new acceptance of people as people instead of as symbols of social status.

▷ **Treboul, near Douarnenez** 1895

Oil on canvas

WHILE ON HOLIDAY at Douarnenez on the Atlantic coast of Brittany, Renoir managed to paint both seascapes and inland pictures. Unlike Monet, Renoir was not particularly attracted by the sea or by landscapes in themselves, preferring to use them as backgrounds for people. Sometimes, however, he made sketches of places that attracted him, rather in the style of a modern holidaymaker taking snapshots for the photograph album.

◁ **The farmhouse at Cagnes** c.1908

Oil on canvas

RENOIR AND HIS FAMILY began visiting Cagnes, in the south of France near Nice, in 1885 and eventually built a house in an ancient olive grove, on the slopes of the hill near the old Grimaldi château. Renoir hoped that the warm winters would help his arthritis and enable him to continue painting – which they did, though his disability, which crippled his fingers and paralysed his legs, was never cured. In Cagnes, Renoir continued to paint almost until his death in 1919 and enjoyed with his family and three sons a near-idyllic family and artistic life. Visitors to his villa at Cagnes, Les Collettes, may still experience something of the idyll in this haven of peace and quiet.

▷ **A View of Cagnes** c.1900

Oil on canvas

THIS VIEW OF CAGNES shows that when Renoir first discovered the small village to the west of Nice and the River Var the area was still very rural. He took an immediate liking to it, and decided it was right for a winter haven where the warmth would help his arthritis. Some years after his first visit in 1888, he began building a house in an ancient olive grove on the slopes facing the hill top and with a view of the sea over fields and woods. The family moved into Les Collettes in 1903. Renoir's property has been preserved much as he left it, and his studio has been furnished with his easel and wheelchair, model's throne and other impedimenta of his working life. The present house (built in 1908) contains many of his drawings and paintings and the ancient olive grove is still there but the view, alas, has mostly disappeared under the concrete of modern developments.

△ **Les Collettes, Cagnes-sur-Mer** c.1908

Oil on canvas

▷ **Portrait of Ambroise Vollard** 1908

Oil on canvas

THE IMPRESSIONIST movement was for some time largely derided by the public, who were used to the old forms of academic art and were unable to understand the new way of seeing the life around them. There were always one or two stalwart supporters of the new painters, one of whom was Ambroise Vollard, a Paris art dealer who became a friend of Renoir in the 1890s and sat for him on several occasions. In this one, he admires a statue by Maillol. Cézanne also did a portrait of Vollard, but his took 100 sittings while Renoir kept Vollard away from his work for a much shorter time.

FOR THE LATTER PART of his life, Renoir divided his year between two properties, spending his summers at Essoyes in Burgundy and his winters at Les Collettes in the south of France near Nice. In 1908 he built his own house at Les Collettes, in the midst of a grove of ancient olive trees. Despite increasing physical difficulties caused by crippling arthritis and rheumatism, Renoir's years at Les Collettes were wonderfully productive, both in painting and in sculpture. Today, Renoir's property at Cagnes-sur-Mer is a museum, allowing visitors a glimpse into the artist's life and the inspiration of some of his greatest work.

▷ **Ambroise Vollard** 1908

Oil on canvas

THERE IS NO DOUBT that
Ambroise Vollard was well
regarded by the Impressionist
painters and that as well as
being their dealer he was a
friend. In a letter to Charles
Camoin, the painter, Cézanne
wrote that the Bernheimes and
another dealer had been to see
him. 'But I remain true to
Vollard.' In his
autobiographical book
'Recollections of a Picture
Dealer', Vollard recounts
many anecdotes about Renoir,
Cézanne and other painter
friends. When he visited
Renoir at Essoyes and asked
him why he lived there instead
of Paris, Renoir replied 'The
butter here is perfect and the
bread better than you get in
Paris. And then there's the
good little vin du pays.'

◁ **Claude Renoir as a Clown** 1909

Oil on canvas

CLAUDE RECALLS in his *'Souvenir sur Mon Père'*, published in 1948 in a book entitled *Seize Aquarelles et Sanguines de Renoir*, that he was very reluctant to pose in the clown's costume in which he appears in this painting. He was particularly against wearing the white stockings his father insisted on because they made his legs itch. There was a long tussle between the father and his young son in which Renoir threatened a spanking for disobedience but in the end had to resort to bribery, promising young Coco an electric train and a box of paints.

▷ **Dancing Girl with a Tambourine** 1909

Oil on canvas

THIS IS ONE of a pair of paintings, the other being a girl with castanets, (modelled by Gabrielle Renard), which was commissioned for the dining-room of M. Maurice Gangnat, one of Renoir's patrons. The exotic character of the subject seems to relate to the *Woman of Algiers* which Renoir had painted in 1870. Then, Renoir saw it as a tribute to Delacroix, but now, 39 years later, perhaps it was just a memory of his youthful visit to North Africa. According to Georgette Pigeot, who modelled for this picture, the girls in both were to have been depicted holding fruit, but the Gangnats decided on the change to musical items, so that the pictures could be hung in other living-rooms.

◁ **Bather Sitting Drying Her legs** 1910

Oil on canvas

BY 1910, RENOIR'S arthritis had grown severe enough to make holding a brush a difficult and painful business. Although he became depressed and threatened to give up painting, he did not give in. When his fingers became twisted and immobilised by the disease, he had brushes strapped to his hand so that he could continue. He not only managed to paint another great version of the *Grandes Baigneuses* but many other nudes, including this version of a girl drying her legs. The richness and luminosity of the flesh tones show that his disability had not affected his sensitive touch.

◁ **Gabrielle with Roses** 1911

Oil on canvas

GABRIELLE RENARD was part of the Renoir family from the time that their second son, Jean, was born in 1894 and took on the roles of nurse, mother's help and model with admirable equanimity. Until then, Aline had been Renoir's in-house model but from now on she appeared as wife and mother in his paintings. In this painting Renoir shows his mastery of both colour and structure and has given it all the solidity and breadth of the old master paintings that he admired so much and had wanted to emulate after his stimulating visit to Italy in 1881. Both Gabrielle and roses were to be used constantly by Renoir as the main inspiration of many of his finest paintings.

ACKNOWLEDGEMENTS

The Publisher would like to thank the following for their kind permission to reproduce the paintings in this book:

Bridgeman Art Library, London /Art Institute of Chicago 14, 15; **/Chateau de Versailles, France** 55; **/Christie's, London** 18, 22, 23, 32, 33, 39, 40, 54, 62, 68-69; **/Courtauld Institute Galleries, University of London** 13, 73; **/Fogg Art Museum, Cambridge, Mass.** 27; **/Giraudon /Musée d'Orsay, Paris** 24-25, 26, 34-35, 38, 42, 47, 58, 64; **/Giraudon /Musée de L'Orangerie, Paris** 75; **/Hermitage, St Petersburg** 59; **/Kunsthalle, Hamburg** 12; **/Louvre, Paris** 78; **/Metropolitan Museum of Art, New York** 28-29, 65; **/Musée d'Orsay, Paris** 48, 49, 56; **/Musée du Petit Palais, Paris** 74; **/Museo de Arte Sao Paulo, Brazil** 77; **/Museum of Fine Arts, Boston, Mass.** 43; **/National Gallery, London** 41, 44-45, 76; **/National Gallery of Art, Washington DC** 20, 21; **/Neue Pinakothek, Munich** 19; **/Palace of the Legion of Honor, San Francisco** 52, 53; **/Philadelphia Museum of Art, Pennsylvania** 50-51; **/Phillips Collection, Washington DC** 36-37; **/Private Collection** 16-17, 30, 31, 61, 63, 66-67, 72; **/Pushkin Museum, Moscow** 10-11; **/Saarland Museum, Saarbrucken** 70-71; **/Wallraf-Richartz Museum, Cologne** 9.